# THE NIGHT JAR

LOUISE PETERKIN

# The Night Jar

SALT

CROMER

PUBLISHED BY SALT PUBLISHING 2020

2 4 6 8 10 9 7 5 3

Copyright © Louise Peterkin 2020

Louise Peterkin has asserted her right under the Copyright, Designs
and Patents Act 1988 to be identified as the author of this work.

First published in Great Britain in 2020 by
Salt Publishing Ltd
12 Norwich Road, Cromer, Norfolk NR27 0AX United Kingdom

www.saltpublishing.com

Salt Publishing Limited Reg. No. 5293401

A CIP catalogue record for this book is available from the British Library

ISBN 978 1 78463 216 8 (Paperback edition)

Typeset in Sabon by Salt Publishing

Printed and bound in Great Britain by Clays Ltd, Elcograf S.p.A

*For The Diggers Writers. You changed my life!*

*In Memory of Paul de Havilland*

# Contents

# THE NIGHT JAR

I open the Night Jar.

The taut lid turning makes the noise of a rock
revolving on the ground.

I collect the materials of the small hours,
all that gorgeous paraphernalia:

the silvered plectrum of a pine cone
a pebble dipped in moon
a chrysalis hanging like tempura

In truth it is a sad vocation
for its solitary nature,

for the things that get inside
and cannot get back out:

the moth with antique wings
the pewter cricket, limbed like a bracelet
the firefly

who guides me home in the dark.
I'm the only soul to have captured a star.

It's like a great rock rolling over
to seal up a tomb

the sound of the Night Jar closing.

# Sister Agnieszka Runs Away to the Circus

Roll up! Big Top in view like a yummy mirage;
scalloped, candy-striped, as good as any church
in scale, in height for the swooping,
the twirling, the leaping and curving
for the love of God, the love
of the falling. The good folk here
fit you for your leotard.
Instructed all day in the fine arts: juggling,
knife throwing, tightrope walking.
You know now balance
is an act of sheer faith,
so spread those arms out in the style of the cross
on a frail bridge above, on the back of a horse.
After work, there is much to enjoy –
a consignment of massive animals,
the Ark-stink of dark and straw.
Lie with the strongman, all night long
if you care to, savour the taste of his body,
his shiny skin, his Colonel Blimp face.
Or console the associates of the sideshow
as they hover towards your implicit grace, soothe them,
let the conjoined twins envelop you like a moth.
Be fearless as you walk that line,
straight across, don't look up or down.
And don't succumb to your nightmare –
you know the one –
where the ground, the trailers,
the skin of the tent tremble,

and you run outside to see
a legion of nuns
come to collect you
come to take you home
lapping at the horizon like an army of penguins,
in their vengeance, Sister,
in their thousands.

# Siren Song

The sleeves of your kimono hang
like the leaves of some gaudy, flesh-eating plant.
There are waffles, syrup. You pour the Colombian –
coffee so rich it has its own weather; clouds, storms
collect on the surface. I sip in my satin.
All made up since six am. Oh God
make something happen. Anything
to break the drone of the morning,
the buzz-cut of flies, the neighbours mowing.
The television casts mutely an actress, gesticulating
like a lobster held aloft by a chef. You flip
through your supplement with a slow tenderness.
You're mumbling something . . .
the merits of sustainable trout fishing.
I'm not listening. I'm watching
as the camera zooms in on a bright apparition,
a young girl beaming from a river bank.
And I think about that drowsy June day
when the dragonflies acupunctured the lake
and you looked up from your boat
bewildered, beguiled
by my smiling and waving
in my best summer dress,
in the teal blue and silver of the afternoon.

# Close

I was always late that summer.
Reckoning it better to call in sick
I drifted towards the lake around two.
Grander, far, far lovelier
to freight whole toupées of weed
through my fingers
and spatterdock and gnats
than to scrape rounds of crud from the broiler.

Frog spawn was bubble wrap on the water.

Ought to have been relief I felt,
thrumming my belly as my body
distilled all its pain and syrupy biology
like a lava lamp.
But I was listless and damp.
My thighs a pair of bellows
slapping out a dark smell of coin
into the sky.

All afternoon the trains clattered on the line.

Back in town, vast mothers reclined
fanning themselves like libertines
on verandas. Calling out
to children with slow loris faces.
I imagined them waving handkerchiefs,
those wide-eyed kids
as I rattled on down the track.
But I wouldn't look back;

no, straight on ahead
stoking the fuel in boiler
orchestrating steam like a barista.

# Ines and the Flood

A committee clustered like an opulent brooch the day the river broke its banks after days of hard rain. A vagrant caught roosting in the church-still rooms of the old Jamieson place. His face at a window startled the children. Now everyone was gunnin' for the guy.

I had bigger fish to fry. Was heading over to Ernest's to give him a piece of my mind. Old bastard had reneged on my promotion. 'Ines', he'd cooed over the phone, 'it was never a foregone conclusion.'

My march was affirmed by the endless torrent and lush shrubs cupping fauna like ornaments. A military beat thundered in my mind. I thought my rage would crack in my throat like glass. As I tried to pass the town hall, the women harried me inside 'Ines,' they hissed 'we need a united front on this.'

I seethed. What harm was he doing? Place had been empty since March. Leave him be. Oh I knew how they thought of me: scrabbly ol' doodle, colours over the edges, like something their kids had splatted out. Now they wanted me to join their bitter union. Well, you know what . . .

. . . down to Ernest's that's what, not to read him the riot act but to buy me a picnic his finest, rankest brandy a ripe cheese fat as a monk under a tree and a ham the size of a cello say hello to this newcomer he sounded alright just my type someone to sail away with like the owl and the pussycat when the rooms fill up and the furniture comes apart like pulled pork and there we'll be bobbing along fishing for jade faces we aren't sure is

money or photographs Ines in love
Ines at sea
Ines, Ines in all that rapture!

# Julie and the Planets

He carries it like a tray precarious with goblets
and still life fruit: careful, ceremonial.
Conserve the vinyl; when treated right
the Saturn discs will fill the room
with a universe. Alone you scatter them,
naked, on the floor, a god
choreographing the planets, enjoying
the clatter like hard liquorice. Look at the lyrics,
sleeve notes for intimacy, study faces
for pockmarks, tight jeans for bulges.
Imagine the studio – ripe and botanical,
the inevitable hash, cola soldering in a bitumen ring.
The engineer high as the moon. The hatreds in heat; sexual.
The guitarists got the lead to put down the vocals again
though it was right, *dammit*, the last time.
You are jerked up like a puppet by a rangy intro,
the cool, spare New Wave at odds
with your shamanistic bopping,
hopscotching records like land mines. Afterwards,
you feel spent, embarrassed. Time to go to work,
dish up eggs and pancakes,
your nylon clinging to blisters like hot plastic.
Watch the jukebox needle dip up and down
like a mechanical chicken.
Meanwhile, he returns
to a silent soundtrack of prior violation,
faint crop circles on the linoleum.

# Don't Go with Fred Ince's Horrible Carnival

And its clown with a face like cracked parchment?
C'mon darling, you can do better. On every shuttered
storefront the posters are leering, wilting at the corners
like hooch-ruined mothers in this squally old Fall.
Do me a favour, next time you saunter down Main Street,
spike a hole through his fat forehead with your stiletto
for me, just you pound it right down on the ground
cos he's a heel and a scoundrel. His ragbag's a sham
for illicit pursuits. Any day now, mark my words
there'll be warrants for his arrest over the flyers –
he's in cahoots with the Mob. I'm looking for a doll,

dumb as polka dot, to sit with aplomb atop a suitcase.
You've heard of a contortionist? They're all the rage in Paris.
This one's the best, a marvel, real rangy –
kind of arms and legs, puts you in mind of a crane fly.
Then he bends, all tucked up in himself like a lawn chair!
You'd do the locks, show the folks in the crowd the key
and (for a bit of theatrics) slip it between your tits.
Smoke a long cigarette for the time it takes
Slim Jim to wriggle free. See, the trick's twofold –
the negotiating of limbs, then the breaking out. You think
you'd get that at Fred's sorry shambles? I'm looking for a dame

who can suss out a charlatan. You've heard of Ince's
World (Ha!) Famous (Ho!) Curiosity Fair? There's an exhibit there:
Tom Thumb's Brain – a marron glacé in a beaker of brine!
All those rotten things he's got bobbing in jars,
the locals lap them up like pissy beer. But this enterprise,
we got our sights on the big time. We're looking for a class act

like you, a real lady. Ince got me once, one time only –
a girl with whom I was to be married. Sometimes
in the star-cold air at the top of the Ferris, I fancy I catch them below
walking hand in hand. Come with me; I'll never let you go.
Don't you want to be kept in grand clothes? Don't you want to see Paris?

# The Mouses

It's not a good sign to imagine the mouses
appearing at the corner of your eye all of your time.
A flick of your hair could cast the effect, or a shadow
sent scurrying by clouds passing over. It's not nice
to kill them either, to poison, see leavings

the colour of electricity cluster in each corner.
Not fair for us to be deities – we're just bigger, our shit
would seem bigger to them like that
of a circus animal. We are dumb, blind, whatever
artefacts we yield of glorious beauty

we undermine; Gregorian choirs line up
like boy bands on album covers. We cheapen
everything or make it meta. It's best not to think
of the layers of croissant, cronut or Paris-Brest
scattering crumbs in all directions to be nibbled

by the mouses. The mouses are not singular;
there's bound to be infestation. I find this hard
to reconcile so I sleep the sleep
of the imbecile, roll and loll and get my fill
until I am headachy and sore then sleep off

these ailments in decrements, digging down
to a pure sleep where the earth is colder
and the ethanol scent of vodka hangs with tubers
like broken light bulbs. But the mouses are still
there, underground, blue as biros, dipping in

and out of bodies like synchronised swimmers.
Even dozing on a sun lounger I saw one,
but it was a piece of pink bougainvillea
rolling to my toes like some robo-pet
a scientist made. Sometimes, I felt the mouses

under tables but it was the cold noses
of feral cats with bones like marimbas. It would
be the worst thing to feel the mouses brush against
your skin; to think of them in motion
is bad enough. Much better to imagine them one

at a time clambering over a mountain of holey cheese
or frozen together in a Christmas card choir
with miniature hats and carol sheets. In the silent night
I hear them scramble for any viable scrap and it's awful
to think of the cronut, the croissant, the mille-feuille.

# Whale

Three days. Three nights.
Echoing a pious little number
through the art installation of my bones and organs.
Delirious, the honed metre of prayer
gave way to feverish incantation,
the O *Fathers* to cries for your *Mother*.
But after a spell you discovered a casket,
a freight of toys and fine wooden carvings.
You rubbed the figures together in the dark.
One of them, dry enough to spark,
blossomed into flame.
Hunched, trembling, you bubbled
the salt from my water,
trailed a flickering light along
an arc of molluscs, glittering clams
hanging like bats
from my pungent cathedral.
You shucked and you sucked,
then scratched three tally marks on my insides with your knife.
Ingrate. You think at God's command I spat you out?
Don't flatter yourself. I couldn't stand
your pacing anymore;
that sorry cacophony through my constitution
gave me indigestion.
I spewed you out into the depths,
the gauzy monsters, the giant squid.
To the slutty old mermaids, green as money.
I knew you would rise eventually,
gasping, sea stinging, sun on your face.
And would live to fight another day, embark

on a zealous campaign.
You preach about your time inside with the fervour of the
reborn.
Still, would you ever allow yourself to truly remember –
with the ebb of the tide, a lavish haul,
when you're gutting a fish for your supper –
the acrid bellyful,
air like a pillow,
that stench, that timbre,
that terrible, familiar
warmth.

# Interview with the Woman who Trepanned Herself

*The brief was to get inside her head.* I fail to chuckle
at the planned intro of my article – too painful –
the ache in my back tooth thumping. I probe inside,
draw out a sewagey smell on my finger. Grab my keys,
Dictaphone, thermos, that slim, constant familiar. Inside
the coffee gleams like the bottom of a drain, coin-glints of sun
through the car window. Backed up in a long colon of traffic,
a pneumatic drill pounding the sidewalk to fragments.

*Can you give our readers an idea why you took such extreme*
*    measures?*
*Would you ever advocate self-trepanation?*
*Why would you powder your cheeks with your own skull?*

Twelve miles out and the houses begin to spread:
twee, robust, occurring like slow blinks.
I've never felt at home in the suburbs, mailboxes like bread tins,
lindens and everything looking so fucking edible.
I found a witch's house when I was little, her front door agape.
I wandered in as if sleepwalking. I remember
the rude-vegetable shape of her nose, inky scribbles round it,
ammonia heavy as talc. Garden shears hung limply at her side,
the broken jaw of some conquered beast.
But she was the one who was bleeding.
I couldn't stop staring.

*Did it hurt?*
*Bullseye. Cyclops. X marks the spot.*
*Hey lady, did the knife thrower miss?*

Why do I take on these freak-of-the-week assignments?
As if there were a choice in the matter, bills pile up,
the rag shirks expenses and all the while THE NOVEL
strains at my forehead: a sad dog at the window.
I need a solid eight hours. Exercise. A yard sale:
some crank last week couldn't open his door for the newspapers
he'd hoarded. In his hovel I stared at a decade. I thought of words
I might have written pulsing at the heart of the tower.
I wanted to let them out.

*Did you experience a kind of spiritual transcendence?*
*Was it like . . . oh, I don't know . . .*
*flying?*

I went to see this guy – doctor's orders – and before I knew it
I was spread, pins sticking out all over me –
a pineapple hedgehog on my mother's buffet table.
I did so want it to work, for the ghosts to flee
from each punctured co-ordinate
with a thwarted hiss and for my brain to go pfffff like a tire.
But it's the same with everything these days, a quick fix –
the sex, hot baths, analysis.
It's like the old-school trick of snatching the table cloth off in one
    seamless swoop –
you're still left with the crockery, the plates,
the empty fruit bowl.

*Is life better now?*
*Do you feel different?*
*How?*

*What was it like?*
*Did it feel like . . . ?*
*Did it feel*
*O*

# Hitchcock

For every jagged coastline cappuccino'd with gull shit
there is a delicate blonde, propelling
to the dark heart in her brittle boat.
For every *Vacancy*
sign bleeding neon into rain,
there is a blonde driving wildly,
on a mad trajectory, all elbows.
The wipers go *eeee eeee*.

I am the architect. I set them on course.
What perils I have in store for my beauties;
the birds and the bell towers,
daggers and doppelgangers,
the hoary Du Maurier seas.
I do a good line in mothers,
with their clammy grips and monstrous wigs,
their pickled walnut faces.

Perhaps in another life
I'd be leading man: Cary Grant or Peck.
For now I am the rebuked, grotesque in my longing,
jowls, my cartoon silhouette.
Maybe I adore the restraint . . .
so pleasurably tense . . .
like trying to get into clothes which are wet.

I tell the girls they'll never work again,
that they're cattle, two a penny.
I'll make them cry. I'll make them
fall in love with me.
I'll bid the birds to pull apart their hairs' embroidery.

# Sister Agnieszka Addresses the Poor and the Needy

For his insolence, for the question
imparted in a long stare up to the terrace
where you perched on a hard chair,
for this impropriety
you punished him justly. Cut his supper
to measly, more of a child's than a horse-

taut man of the fields. The chastisement was apt,
for he was a glutton, the way he bolted
down the stew and the dumplings,
letting all the garlicky ghosts out of the trapdoors.
He could not bring himself to ask for more,
such was his pride. You relished

his balk at the plate, it keened you.
Inside you were cold, honed, slim as a knife.
Still, the inference remained, echoed for days
in the Rome-cool tunnels of the convent,
the ordered garden. Words unspoken,
conveyed in his gaze:

*How can it be enough, Sister?*
*This trowel of soil? Or the sunlight*
*worn on your back like hair . . .*
*flowers, chores, helping the poor . . .*
*this timetable of prayer?* Audacity!
Yet a doubt crept under your skin.

So when he looked up suddenly from kissing your breast
as if you had in that very moment spoken,
he looked so plain-faithed and searching,
that you pushed his head back down,
as if he could mend your heart.
For you were quite sure then it was broken.

# O Chorizo

Chop it this way: the horseshoe clean
down the middle, half in the fridge for later.
Now peer into its universe, gemmed and celled
with fat and paprika. Anatomy of a stout wee genie.
Is it so very bad for me? Yes!
you chuckled. I was in the kitchen
dicing the stuff up in a kitsch little apron
when you wrapped your arms round me from behind
sneaked a chunk into your mouth, kissed me.
Felt like I was in a 50s sitcom,
one about a housewife and a vampire:
*Once Bitten . . . The Bloodsucker Next-door . . .*
Of course it was cancelled. I still buy it;
I like its butch taste. The garlic, the pearls, and the ochre.
The way it stains everything, the way it stains my fingers.

# Brazil

Summer as thick as foliage, the city in waves,
haze; rank, sweet bins. Through neglect
or lack of imperative, I'm overgrown
like a garden. The hair comes up like worms.

There was a time I was shiny. Burned
from plucking, waxing, depilatory cream.
Bald as Mattel's finest. Sore, spurned,
the lonely go to seed in a summer bereft

of the sea, a slice of exotica. Remember
the boat? Green horizon, hammock of heat.
A man with a face like raw chicken
visored his eyes with his hand to see

the island where the potent frogs were tiny,
where the birdsong jangled like jewellery. Is it you
I miss? Or that sensuality? I'm overgrown.
The hair comes up like revolutionaries.

# Perfume

We drowned the flowers

in a plastic tub already kissed
with the three flavours of Neapolitan.

Kneeling in a garden striped with shade,
extracting

fuchsia tongues. We tugged
the folds from a tea rose

till all that remained was rust
on bare leaves like cigarette burns.

We let it steep for two weeks
in the shed's dark corner.

When it was ready
we opened the lid to a tomb,

black sludge edging the inside:
a necromantic border.

We hid our horror at the slime,
baptised the fetid pong, "Parisienne"

and in emptied shampoo bottles
labelled over with a flouncy script

distilled the sullied water
for our mothers.

# Renfield

Not entomology, nor some god-aping
yen for a menagerie to bend to my will
but for the blood, the lifeblood sir! It flows
through the strata of the littlest things.
I was precious

at first, reticent. So when a bee marred
itself in a clumsy descent from the window
I let it curl for days like a dried flower
before I sampled. I smiled:
it tasted liverish, autumnal.

> I dusted the sill with sugar for a fly
> I blackened the sill with flies for a spider
> The spider would tempt down a bird

But I was impatient; I indulged.
I rattled a flea to my ear
then popped it in my mouth like a pill.
My fingers took on the tang of a bell,
faint arcs of gore under each nail

as if I had been playing a black pudding piano.
Small viscera
hung from my gums like a piñata.
I needed self-control if I wanted the sparrows!
I began once again to propagate.

Until the day the doctor entered my cell
to find the air and my hair full of birds.
And what he conveyed, not so much in words
but a sharpening glint in his eyes was a sort of . . .
respect. I wouldn't say awe. No, not just yet.

# Notable Globsters
*According to Wikipedia*

include the Stronsay Beast. Measuring in at some 50 feet minus tail – missing by all accounts. Sea serpent! cried the anatomists, citing its length and wing-like protrusions. But no, it was the remains of a basking shark crudely recast by the bloom and curtsey of rot to this: a magic carpet unfurled on the beach, a stinking stretch of mass pimped up with the Jurassic swellings of decay. But what of the witness who affirmed it had fur, that it glowed?

And what of the St Augustine Monster, washed up on the coast of East Florida? Boys on their bikes caught its glint in the distance: an aircraft crash-landed and smashed on the shore. On closer inspection: a punctured hot air balloon, tethers hacked off, the Humpty Dumpty head subsiding to blancmange, a pink white exhalation of breath, a smelly rude noise. The implication was clear from the severed stumps: this thing would have had tentacles, huge, eight in number, perhaps sundered in a violent demise. Octopus gianticus! But no, the collagen was decreed vertebrate, most likely that of a sperm whale.

So, for pity's sake, save us all the Garonne Chanson! Hugged by the reeds now and nuzzled by catfish till its scrappy increments detach in a buff cloud. When it's trawled up time-spoiled and reeking it will be subject to a media flashing like dragonflies, forensics, intense cogitation. Its alarming shape could be explained away by the usual transmutations of putrefaction. But no microscope's eye will decipher the swatches of DNA, no-one will quite find words to describe its colour. And when someone in the crowd asks why was the carcass singing? nobody will give a definitive answer.

# The King who Ate Himself to Death

But it was Fat Wednesday and soon to be Lent.

But the blowhard lobster was centrepiece; his magnanimous claws
said, "pull up a chair".

But the kippers came trussed up in pairs – co-dependent Pisces,
perfectly ichthyomorphic! Sharing two eyes,
lips melded to a fountain spout.

But the weeks ahead to go without.

But the sauerkraut!

But there was a compelling visage
on tin-glazed earthenware. I had to eat
to reveal the plate's gaze.

But the caviar winked like hawthorns.
The hawthorns were hulled like monarchs for schnapps.

But not a wince as the champagne
was sapped, so smooth it was, and perfumed.

But the turnip was smashed on letter-thin crispbread,
sweet and ear waxy.

But a funky, wise pig head was cobbled to brawn, fanned
out like a card deck on white Chinese porcelain.

But the sauces of gin, the sauces of cherry.

But the candles guttered like history.

But each pretty twinned kipper
held a hot hunk of butter!

But the fourteen dishes of semla

But the fourteen dishes of semla:
almond cream filled,
corroding swaddles in raisin-steeped milk.

But I thought there was time ahead still
to recompense,
day after day after day

# Pertussis

Nothing can be done; this ailment sounds straight out of Homer;
a fringed and wingèd creature unleashed on the somnolent world.
Contagion's stalled by a run of antibiotics
then you're on your own.
You feel *awful*. Feudal. Oddly scatological
though it's all up here in the bone cage –
perhaps a drop lower –
from a pitch pit that resounds in a throat chirr,
the terrible hacking. You aren't just coughing. You are heave-
heave ho-ing
molluscy tokens in the sink and toilet,
reading yourself like tea leaves in the dream-coloured mucus.
You always hated the guys who imitated coffee percolators,
hawking thick globules on street corners.
Now you're greasing the world like a snail.
You are wretched and retching.
You're that dog from Wacky Races.
You are splat.
You are whooping.
And it feels like the sum total of all your indignities.
When the right words were out of your grasp
or corked in your throat as you bottled it,
you took to the stage and the words stopped
                        here.
And when they came out they weren't what they were.

# If Ines

was in a fairy tale she would still have a good for nothing, dumbass father, 'cept this one would be in some caca-coloured tunic and hose, shoes with buckles big as toads instead of the Bojangles' Famous Chicken n' Biscuits t-shirt he got that one time from the Coliseum in Charlotte. Point being: he would forsake her in a heartbeat – maybe to save his own skin after trespassing in the garden of the Beast, trying to steal a cutting of swamp milkweed. *You're no lepidopterist!* Beast would exclaim. No, her father would sigh, looking down at the steed-frayed ground, *but I do have a daughter pressed inside glass.*

∽

If the barflies and busybodies asked he would justify his actions – *who else would have her?* There were those who thought Ines peculiar because she chose to engage in useful pursuits like counting the teeth inside her head with her tongue and troubling caterpillars' parts till they turned into gluey accordions. In storms, she was prone to say things like, *Can a body be rained on to death?* If Ines were in an old time novel this would be considered melancholy but as things stood the townsfolk eyeballed her as she daydreamed on the corner of Woodruff; the fawn coloured mutt at her side barking itself empty in the midday downpour.

∽

Beast was never where you expected. If Ines climbed the staircase to his porch, he snarled from stage left in the heliotrope; teddy in an attic's ebb, fuzzy wuzzy king of no see ums, glider-set, nursing his growls and a Singapore Sling. She watched his cowed bulk at garden's end where the hybrid roses held their hands up, grooming his horse in circular motions like a boy buffing a car. He got down on one knee, clutched a smouldering hoof in his paw. Ines only cried twice during her stay; when she thought the wine poached pear for dessert was a squab sitting in a pool of its own blood. And when she thought Beast was going to produce a ring.

∾

If Ines could pin a tail on when her feelings changed. She hated the house at first with its candelabras like weeping willows and mantle clocks mounted on lion claws; gold tainted with verdigris like dead crabs washed up on the shore. Beast didn't care for some of her amusements like when she stalked little creatures through the halls in her stockinged feet or studied their smears in the traps she'd set. One day, he opened his mouth (it was black and plush like the inside of Firebird) and a wren shot out. Beast said *I know that deep down there's beauty inside you*. Ines was touched, though part of her found it a bit rich.

∾

If only Ines could decide what to do with her father! Her time with Beast had afforded her a new-found poise (look at her riding down the fold, side saddle!) The rust-whipped hold pogoed into view, overgrown with machinery like dusty, bloody rhinos. Ines tethered the horse and peered through the window overgrown now with big-headed plants which resembled Audrey 11. She saw her father throned on a lawn chair reigning over flayed chicken and bones – the sovereign of an obscure country whose name is not quite a palindrome. Forgiveness came like the rain.

# For Ratatouille

To release their sweetness you must
violently undress them.
So the Wicked Witch toes
of two Romano peppers curl up in the heat,
the oven set to singing.
And I'm away, banging drawers in the kitchen
for cellophane in which the charred swag
should steam and sag until – grim magic –
the skin comes loose. Neat and clean.
I douse them under a cold tap –
these scorched Bota bags
(they're how the stepmother pictured Snow White's
mined heart, scarlet and ebony,
hot as the Big Bang).
The outer slips off under running water,
the ribbed flesh squids my fingers.
A saga of seeds follow like roe.

And there you go – kingly,
admiring your emptied plate,
remarking on their intensity.
How could you know
the bubble and flay
of their martyrdom?

The remnants clog the drain
like a novelty condom.

# Kay

I emboss your dreams with diamonds,
with corridors of ice,
and a soft frayed mile of white,

a see-through throne with a haar around,
a floor, a door
a long thin sliver of light.

Fortunate child, to you I bestow
an arch of stars,
delicate trappings;

the intricate spectre
of a shimmering fountain
suspended in motion.

You do not know me.
In sleep, you play in my fortress,
dragging your sleigh behind in a glitter trail.

Upon waking, you never tell
yet break from the crowd
to stare into the distance.

You shiver. I'm closer.
When I come for you,
you will hear bells.

# Snake

No one suspected I could be so snakey.
By the time they found his body
it was too late;
all the police could do was loop yellow tape
where the door had been. I was long gone.
My skin like hosiery on the floor.

I nudged to the east with panache.
But like the stones that studded my path,
the bones that revised my digestion
to a kind of archaeology, there were clues:
sodden shirts twisting
round my arm like a bracelet,
the spiced tomb of the laundry basket.

How lithe I am I have wriggled free!
I hiss like Peter Lorre. A small bird
fizzes like seltzer inside me.
Who would have thought I could be so snakey?
His face was all inky with poison.
Like a sewing machine,
I had punctured him in a great many places.

# Project: Gingerbread House

Those in the know will tell you –
windows are hardest:
syrup boiled and spread
into flat slick squares
to cool in the shade of a plum tree.
Eased from workbench to frame
by Bill and me: two clods
straight outta Buster Keaton. So delicate
her toad just has to look at it
for it to shatter. Liquorice is better,
more pliable, strong enough
to plait into rope for the guttering.

From her interim shack the old bag clanks,
scratching her crotch in a sullied kimono.
An angular foreman, she sucks a cheroot,
makes tyrannical demands at the roof
with her talons
                          – Bigger chimney!
        Twice the marzipan!
One thing's for sure
she wouldn't be nowhere without our artistry.
Bill got a killer recipe for fruit loaf from his Nan,
dense as a mob-heavy, water resilient.
Foundation's the key,
the rest is just froufrou:
candy cane fencing,
rococo wig of white piping.

I come home an albino, dusted with sugar.
My wife is resentful: my lack of libido,
stupefied grin. I'm getting cuddly.
The kids waft towards my smell:
caramel and first, warm milk.
They hang off me like pelts on a fur.

Bill got mugged by bees yesterday;
the house transfers honey like a kiss,
his skin was gummy as a postage stamp.
Battle-axe said she had a balm for the stings,
took him inside. That was the last I saw.
A plume of sweet smoke rose to the sky.

I went out in the woods but got sleepy,
looked up where the trees ringed round
a cauldron of blue. The ground's mouldy reek
gave me cause to remember:
tang of manure, the latrine's
big punch in the kisser.
I had a hankering then:
for a hunk of strong cheese like a varicose vein,
for the crook of my wife's elbow.
But she was already calling me back.

The house had the lure of a carnival.
O toffee apple cotton candy zephyr.

# Glory

Old Alexandra, fretful as a candle. It's no use,
your voice shot to hell; might as well open the window,
scream into the gales. To save my brain I switch

you off. Night night old budgie, sleep tight. At lights out –
uterial symmetry of your harrowed face, bivalve, after-
image of carved pumpkin, Rorschach test. Joined at the hip

as girls, blonde and curly cherubs of the pillow-fighting ilk,
secrets fizzed between us like sherbet. We'd split
a coke at the movies, pass the spittle straw to and fro. The Glory

stood on Prospect then; the screen flickered like a fireplace.
Could've caught alight, the hairdos of the patrons, ablaze
in the spectral blast where the dust motes did an allegro. We'd watch:

the scroll and the silage, the slumbering dormouse
of a lady's coiled bun. Bet she was a governess, no nonsense,
though the kids tried her tensile with their horseplay. Or perhaps

she was wed to the man on her left with the broken tonsure
gleaming like a bedsit basin; would his head smell like rubber
or mozzarella pooling in a bowl? After the film we'd share

wonton soup, our two spoons disturbing the petrol spill
of sesame oil on the surface. We'd go Dutch,
whoever faced the waiter would slurp

him up with big eyes. In those days our hair was our glory.
You snapped the cookie. *You will burn the town down.*
I laughed, Alex, but look at us now –

skulls corrugated under marsupial wigs;
the haystack girls, batty as a tangle of knitting.
Dangerous too, our penchant for arson. But that was then;

we've had our fun. Tonight I play records
and you dream you are young. The Glory
heads are turning: voiceless, bald as thumbs.

## Sister Agnieszka *is* Carmine Revenge
*(after Muriel Spark's Reality and Dreams)*

Stand on that hill, the director says,
like a strawberry-scented switchblade,
splayed, you know the kind, propped up
for a retail shot on wegotknives.com.
Spread those legs and stand on that hill
like Modesty Blaise, your hands on your hips.
He keeps pointing, angling his head
but there is no hill,

only a screen of green
from floor to ceiling. He hovers on his crane
as she ascends the scaffold. A novice,
hurled into this business, not from obscurity
but from a life starred with beauty
earned by her vigilant eye, a gift
the Buddhists call Bodhi. On meeting
the director she noticed his hands, dictating

the air round her coif, flat palms slicing,
miming a box for her face – a canvas, blank,
already framed. He pulled out a lipstick,
in three slick swathes painted a mouth
over her mouth. Now she stands –
in a studio just south of Pinewood, her trailer
downwind of the portaloos. Starlet, muse, smile
the colour of rage:

Carmine Revenge.
*Her name in the blood of a thousand cochineal*:
the tagline would ooze on posters
in moth-gnawed theatres beside saunas
and vape stores. Sister climbs down for a fag break,
swats away the makeup team like gnats.
She considers the girl in the catering van,
her greasepaint, the perfume of tallow. A grace

to her application, dedication to the craft
of flipping, anointing grey burgers
with red snogs of ketchup. A crane fly
sizzles to a hiss on the grill. The director
calls the crew to set by megaphone. O
He who must be, architect, creator
of this creature feature –
Daddy longlegs.

# Blofeld's Lair

This was the Devil's house. We rent it out now
for super villainy and such. Extinct?
It's up for debate if a volcano ever truly is;
this only adds

                                   a certain frisson

to the layers of jeopardy
that constitute our job description.
The magma chamber's long since cooled
to pluton, the earth's deep interior
tie-dyed, shades of desert and vulva,
Hiroshima shadows of peacock. It's hard to tell
from his stark grey garb and pale moon head
but the boss has an eye for aesthetics. Look!
In gilded frames: Bosch's depiction of Hell
as Byzantine carnival, Bouguereau's damned
giving each other terrible love bites.
Each morning we stand to attention

                                   as he glides

the monorail to his black leather chair.
(I ordered that! Reclining, six castors.
I think of comfort, ergonomics.) He never looks
at us, strokes the white Persian on his lap.
I think he must be shy.
I want to trace his monocle of scar,
tell him I like working here so far,
sure beats the maisonette with mother,
the sideways rocket of her iron lung, CV of years,
turning the chenille cushion wet as well-rope with my tears.
Here, every day is a new adventure.

                                 I glance up

to where ninjas dangle like Spanish moss from trees
and the hydraulic steel hatch

                              opens

its cool lid to a sliver of blue.
A word of advice for those too timid
to make a leap – remember
it's only the ones you know who can hurt you;
the ones you love, you have to fear.
Beware rogue agents in tuxes, their charm
and their pistols. There's a comfort in belonging,
in donning the same, plain uniform. Look!
The silver screens slide open
to the marked world, the UN,

                              a shark aquarium.

# Jaws

Nothing's too strong for me to get through:
iron chains, barbed wire, I gnaw bullets
like al dente pasta, munch on jugulars;
a bouncer Dracula waxing lyrical about
the vena cava. In my head, that is,
though being mute's of no consequence –
in the midst of abject solitude, music persists:
song of the can opener, car crusher,
pig squeal of impossible compact,
dental bur and all the lovely bells and whistles
of the abattoir, henna-tipped, dangling.
Call me lackey if you like, brute, lurching
my seven foot plus bulk towards a victim on cue,
a Minotaur gait, unstoppable, oddly dapper
in belt and braces. But I've a bent towards subtlety,
the detection of notes on a lily-
white nape . . . plumeria, sweet pea, skin flora,
all the usual secretions fear brings to sap.
I joined a dating agency . . . *tall, dark, dependable* . . .
Clutching a showy bouquet in the middle
of the bustling station like a towering statue,
children looking up, astounded, tourists snapping.
Should know better than to open my mouth. We never
make it to dinner, my *killer smile* flashing
like a shoal of mackerel. Well, if my lot
in life's to die alone, so be it. In the daily grind –
crushing hard composite to powder, feeling
the larval throb of pulse against my lips –
I appreciate the basics, the mineral
beginnings of things. In the end, I doubt

I am so very different from others – always
someone else giving the orders, always
the taste of blood in my mouth.

# Aviary

*for Monsieur Robert-Houdin*

Inventory of tiny automata; I tap your heads, faucet cold.
Little clocks, awaken! Colour of the Argonauts.
*Brrr brrr*, stir and preen, incline towards the potted tree
that swells real fruit in magic time; part eclipse, part

burlesque, orange blossom unfurl like wings. I grow
each year in the eyes of my peers yet scrape knees
climbing oaks, trying to harness your song's cagey pitch.
In a temper fit I christen you: Death! War! Famine! Pestilence!

I have the patience of the watchmaker, the watchmaker's
elven fingers. In a far land revolution's deterred by my
conjuring. But my museum's all a twitter; the birds
nudge nudge wink wink. There is conspiracy,

a cabal of torsion springs like wormholes, cogs, mechanisms
cool as cool eggs, cheekbones. Voyeurs at an accident,
the chill birds turn their heads. Bronze beaks open, a plaintive
   trill:
*Call us Raphael! Call us Michael! Call us Gabriel! Call us Uriel!*

# My Father's Sci-Fi

Hard backed, jam-packed in condiment colours: cocktail sauce,
Colman's Mustard. A sepia tang rose from inside, pages the
colour of old men's fingers. Time travel of deflated prices: 80p
for a novel, more in US/ Canadian dollars. Kneeling at the shelf
behind the sofa I fought the tedium of long afternoons slack
as space; the drowsy clock; sear of sad, squandered sun on my
back. My father lay dozing. Sometimes, his snoring would
stop and I counted the s e c o n d s a sick fear he was dead
making my toes tingle. Only his Norse blasts resuming released
my own breathing, the task of the antiquarian. Philip K. Dick.
*Dune*'s sprawling dynasty. Asimov's mysteries – taut and lovely
– a box of gems held up with tweezers in a stark white light,
the jeweller a squinting cyclops. I liked Bradbury, collections
compiled from 50s magazines. The best story hurled me

like a pod from a spaceship into a vacuum of infinite dark
folded onto itself like velvet with absolutely no

stars. A man on a long haul space flight. He was convinced his
sole companion, Wilbur, was an android, assigned to save his
mind from the crumble of solitary confinement. Wilbur was
detached, aloof, impersonal. Our narrator: charismatic, inquis-
itive, jovial.

Then they switched him off. They. Switched. Him. Off. The
narrator was the robot all along.

That was a kick in the guts.

That was when I realised there were stairs in my head and I had to stare straight ahead not to tumble down them, get smashed at the bottom.

The covers were frightening: A prickly jewel stared out from one, a sort of pincushion with eyes hanging in a sea of yellow. The worst was a man with a bald head cracked at the top like a boiled egg, out of which rose a moth. The moth rising out of the man's head had a man's head. And it was bald as an egg, cracked at the top with a moth rising out. The moth had the face of a man's bald egg head, cracked . . .

## You Are Cordially Invited to the Home of Henry Phillips Lovecraft, on His 6th Birthday

There will be jellies, huge as pavilions, in the flavours
of blood blister, ectoplasm, alien. Mother
piles the flufferrnutters on the table.
To compensate for my hideousness,
we must pull out all the stops. A grief to her:
the long, wrong bones of my face: sullen, viscous,
horsey in repose. It's why we don't step outdoors,
though the New England air is crisp as laundry,
asters blazing like galaxies. My party
shall have the taint of a wake;
scudding black drapes of mourning ladies
pushing chairs against walls – dissonant
Big Blink of space. In the dim room
pothos writhes round the frames, black flowers
pucker to mouths. O, if they come
I will run up the stairs
to a rose gold place where silence resounds like a bell
(I stand in the aftermath: tremulant, thrilled.)
Grandfather's library – I have gobbled it up,
have found within doors
to unthinkable worlds: Grimm,
Ovid, Arabian Nights. Dripping into my sleep –
illustrations from Paradise Lost –
they make my brain throb like a meteorite. I dream
of a creature below our front porch, boneless,
white eyes roaming its circumference
like billiard balls, squelching, gaining slow,
sticky purchase in the perfumed dark. I dream
of the boatman plunged into water. He emerged
changed, a genuine Frog King; the river's providence

hanging off him in tendrils. I dream of the old one
at the foot of the ocean, his jade, outland mass,
tangled thrash of tentacles, his horrible patience.
I'm afraid of my visions. In this house
of shadows, death and insanity brush
against my cheek. It is inevitable
such things will come to pass. I remember
how Grandfather cured me of my malady –
I stumbled blindly from room to room
rehearsing an immunity to the dark. Very well.
Mother, when they come,
when they ring the bell, answer,
let them in: all the contemptuous gods,
all the old ones, all the terrible
jellies of the universe.

# Indiana Jones and the Narrow Escape

How could you ever be the settling down type?
For once, this is you being totally honest;
you hold my gaze, my head in your hands like a holy relic.
It's not just the lifestyle: the rolling boulder
over a rope bridge rickety mine shaft coaster
of it all. It's the nature of your closest shaves; your nightmares
are of confinement, the walls closing in like autograph hunters,
a ceiling dripping spikes . . . No matter that it's me
who's got you out of a few jams . . .
Don't laugh! I may have stepped on the off-switch
accidentally but if I hadn't you'd be Panini by now!
If you must know, my therapist says I should dump you,
that this relationship has beset me with a most singular anxiety.
Sure, there are things I could do without. Nazis.
The constant threat of kidnap and peril. Being hurled
from one far off locale to another –
Shanghai to a throbbing Moroccan market
without so much as a change of clothes or Imodium.
It's just that each time I think this must be the last, that –
please God – you must be done.
But there's always another treasure, some ancient booty to discover.
Haven't you learned? Those who have witnessed
first-hand the gilt of the uncanny,
who've brought the spoils to their lips, they've all melted to a puddle,
crumbled to dust! You should know by now,
there are things we mustn't meddle in . . . Oh yes, I forgot,
it isn't the prize. It's the chase. The quest.
Can you not just live in the moment?
Even on a plane I see your mind's eye wandering,
winding a trail through an aerial map in leathery tan,

wishing away the miles, tossing whole continents behind you.
What is it about commitment that scares you – even more than snakes?
Perhaps it's the stillness, sitting in your chair like a knight guarding the
    Grail,
watching the slipping of time in the drifting motes. I remember
that precarious dangle – the top of the tomb sealed by villains,
KerPlunked with shafts of light and the floor alive
with serpents. Writhing. Seething. You were terrified.
At the time I thought I was too. But now I look back,
I could have hung like that for eternity,
just you and me between above and below,
holding on to each other, holding on to the rope.

# The Forgotten Mad Scientist

searches for mob light like a child
scans the night sky for fireworks; torchlight
and a quickening on the brow of the furthest hill
(behind which a village spills like kismet). He looks for
these hostile first-footers, best wool work slippers on,
dressing gown: ornate, oriental. Lancets are fanned
out on the table, the door to his fizzy lab – ajar.

The skeleton staff here are part of the furniture:
the pale butler's a whittled flute, carrying his pain like a tray,
the ghost ship of the maid floats in with the supper plate
and a fork with two tines as this is olden times
and the moor is a pitch void which relies on          mob light
to spark any real sense of vector from here to there,
horde to castle, proletariat to lair. The Scientist considers

the snuggled up together bones of radius and ulna,
the nifty pineal sending out missives to rise and shine.
He elects to dull his thoughts with Moldovan wine,
descends to the cellar, cartouched with cobwebs,
chambered and tiered like a hive. Therein lies

his experiments, a stunted orchard of man parts,
skin flaps covering mouths and groans
like the umber, cheesy bandages of war.
He would give his life for the stone foundations
to rumble with an oncoming charge. Or for just one
solitary figure on the horizon, patchwork and stoic –

he would hold out his palm to him like tundra.

# First Term at Saint Rose of Lima's

Dear Mother,

It is customary for the girls to receive packages which they score with Swiss army knives. Their pale hands shake. Often, the brown paper is stained. They pull out the goods like midwives, hold them up to bulbs which quiver so above the stark dormitories it's as if they have a covering of fur. We can barely contain our excitement but are sure to be patient: the crux of the ritual is to wait until midnight.

Of course the staff know something's afoot. Why, only yesterday didn't I catch a crafty half-smile slip off Mam'zelle onto the floor, right up to Matron's jolly old face! Such good sports; their complicity adds to the wheeze.

Then that hallowed hour where moonlight slides in like cinema on the cache of tins. We peel open sardines in tomato sauce like blood. Pineapple rings and spam. Jars of crystalized ginger bobbing in dark suspension like honeycomb.

Oh Mother, though I do miss our home, I think I should be very happy here.

Your darling, loving
Daughter.

~

Dear Mother,

I'm sorry it's been over a week since my last letter. Promise not to worry – I'm consigned to the sanatorium till I recover. This beastly belly ache! I can barely glide pen over paper, tight as I am in starched, white sheets. I must say, Matron's been an absolute brick, swooping in and down with her spoon every now and then. Mother, please don't think I have acquired airs – but the fact is even the castor oil tastes heavenly here, like when you are going out to dine and kiss me goodnight and I catch the lovely perfume in your hair.

Mummy, I must sign off now as I feel rather queer . . .

My dreams are so strange. I wish I could describe them but forget them as soon as I wake.

Take care Mother!

Much love,
Daughter.

~

Mother,

Something rather odd occurred during lacrosse (I don't mean to sound haughty but it is such a silly game, wafting those big nets above our heads like we are trying to catch giant butterflies).

Anyway Mummy, here's the thing. When Dunny blew the half-time whistle I saw a strange youth beckoning me over from the wire fence. I took one look at his shabby clothes and rope-for-a-belt slouch, knew without doubt he was a bad sort. But there was something about his eyes . . . so deeply brown, undulating with a fawn-like sincerity. His face was as white as a washroom tile as he drew his mouth close to my ear, whispered:

*There's a war on*

When I asked old Dunny about it she just gummed my mouth with a lemon wedge, pushed me into the flurry of panting girls.

Mummy, what did he *mean*?

Anxiously awaiting your answer,

Your doting Daughter.

∾

Mother,

I'm told I am a woman now.

Though I smouldered scarlet like that old brick in a sock we kept for chill nights, Matron insisted on showing everyone how to apply the napkin and belt. As the girls circled, I tried to imagine the contraption she took out as a cheerful invention; a parachute, a fairy hammock. But as I stepped in I thought this is how it would be if Houdini's shackles were elastic. Mother, it looked all the world like a straitjacket.

The pain drips nightly like jam through muslin. The bedsheets are stained.

It's a rotten lot to be grown up!

From your Daughter, with love.

≈

Dear Mummy,

Two weeks and no news . . . I dare say you're frightfully busy; knitting, the WI and the whippets. I feared a postal strike but only this morning another hamper arrived. Lettie's great-aunt from Kettering; a big round of tea cake, condensed milk, peaches. Lately, my appetite is waning. The girls tuck in with gusto, marmalade glossing their chins like flower sap. From where I stand in the corner, they look quite mad – flaxen heads bunching, grey bottoms seesawing round the yummies.

Mummy, their eyes gleam. They use words like *lashings*.

I have come to the conclusion that eating at midnight is bad for the digestion.

Please write soon! Do! Do!

Love always,
Daughter.

∼

Mother,

I did something wicked.

Sleepless, I crept out the dorm in the middle of the night, saw light where Mam'zelle's door was ajar. I heard laughter, peered in to see her and Matron sat round a glistening chicken, plucking it like a harp, feeding each other. They had a marvellous fire going; all was radiant, as if Rumpelstiltskin had spun straw into gold from floorboard to rafter.

Matron sucked on Mam'zelle's finger.

I was just so blasted tired of boiled ham with its bolero of jelly. Next morning I sneaked in to plunder that carcass, the bones like quills, hairy with meat. Daily, I go to the shipwreck; the flesh on the turn, redolent of strawberries.

I simply cannot wait for the holidays.

Please write back soon Mummy
and forgive

your
Daughter.

P.S. In Mlle's grate amongst the ashes: bits of newspaper, hand-writing, scrap of postage stamp: unicorn de-horned by the char. I intend to piece these findings together till they make a lick of sense. I know, I know, if only I spent as much time on my algebra as deciphering funny codes I would far and away be school swot! You should see me Mummy, in the witching hour, on cold wooden boards, trying to spell out Eternity!

∾

Dear Mother,

The girls have sent me to Coventry. This is not at all a good thing despite the lovely trip we took there two summers back – even Aunt Ginny marvelled at the cathedral!

They say I am a goose and conceited. I ask too many questions. Above all, they say I am not a sport; the worst thing to be, I mean, the worst thing not to be.

They needed to take me down a peg or two. Was just a jape really. Suppose I had it coming.

I was sleeping deep as I have been of late, the same dream where I come to the high gate. On the other side, shimmering in the grass, is a silver key – like the one on a tin of pilchards. I use my lacrosse net to get under, swoop it towards me.

Then I break free. Run for miles over swelling, surging green.

I awoke to find the bed sticky; the girls had stolen a specimen from biology, put it in my sheets. Even after a boil wash, there's still a shadow of frog like a trampled autumn leaf.

Mother, I thought that the heartbeat was in my feet.

Darling Daughter.

∾

Dear Mother,

I passed a note to the shabby young man (I think he may be a gypsy). It said:

*What is happening?*

I paced by the fence, waiting for him

The girls    staring at me from east wing tower window.  I sense they sense    deceit.

Mother, my bad hands are greasy with meat.

D x

~

Mother,

Where are you? Where are your letters?

What do these words mean?

Occupied
Air raid shelter
Rationing

Who is this man pointing with big moustache? He *needs* me.
Who is this man with little moustache?
 (Please find cuttings enclosed)

How is my father?
        How is my brother?

Where are your letters?

Daughter.

～

Dearest Mother,

For days now     weak to get out of bed.

I try to    move    am sticky to sheets.

  The Girls   come   at me   in          waves

like the moonlight     I hear the pad of feet        swoosh of
nightgowns
                    The girls come at me as if in          waves
but I have the one      eye
                open

                    always            have this fever

the dream where
I make clear I make

clear

of the fence but the wire cuts in above my thigh ripppsss the
skin  it flows out of me mummy: myself    myself        till I am
too tyred to go further and that's wheyre thay catch me jusst
passstt the wyre
            I love you Mummy but I must        stooppp

forever

Daught

# Pranzo

*Rucola! Ru-co-la!* The chef's hot charges
blare like a klaxon: His mania is theatre here,
the kitchen on view – de rigueur –
and each pale lackey's misdemeanour: the addition of
brandy to the pan. Applause from the tables for his shouts,
for the flame's mauve hissy fit. No escaping it,

he's what the tourists are paying for: some local colour.
The workplace a bachelor's hovel: low strips of pasta
hang overhead like long johns.
Masseur with a grudge, he pummels the dough for pizza,
fingers branded with garlic,
chopping board whorled with tomato.

After service he harries through the plaza
scattering children like pigeons.
He feels it always; his poor heart straining, a sensation
akin to a crush but it's really just rage's carnal urgency.
By a high, cool window he spoons his mother luncheon.
Her sweet face sets with Botticelli resignation.

# Eurydice

Find me my darling. Hone into the underworld
as if nose-diving into the workings of a clock:
compound, blink-clear lines
around its grooves and cogs. Teeming,

the city is a classical font, vibrating,
then erupting with insects.
Nobody looks at each other
though we split and multiply like cells or hysteria.

The cars come out of nowhere.
The lights are always red.
And I'm the lab rat in the labyrinth.
I'm here. No, *here*. No, hither.

Could I ever be at home in this place?
With its Gothic spirals, its damp cathedrals,
that impress to the touch like a corpse.
Fall into the underworld like a wish into a well.

I shall enlighten you on the nature of Hell –
It's not sulphur, pitchforks, brimstone
but tarmac, roadworks, a timetable.
It's grey, my love, quite grey. But manageable.

# Jean Harlow, Black Dahlia, Norma Jean

Who's pissed in the snow?
Hoodlums! And yet,
you can't slice a woman
like a bee or a rose –
the stem broken, sting sliding off
in a gluey exaggeration. Remove
your antebellum garb – harvest hat
and secateurs – there will be no
snapping

in half
of flowers and insects, a most
nubbiny bisection; a tumble of bits
to fall at your feet like potpourri
or mollusc meat, and all with a
green milt gush! The damage requires
the elbow grease
of a butcher,
several black bin liners

in an echoey bathroom,
white-tiled
to give the splashings of blood
an art deco accent; yellowed
grouting like cervical margins.
Marilyn plastered her face with hormone cream –
it had the sheen
of soft peach fur. We can rifle
through the cabinets of the beautiful-

famous
but in the end we are staring
at the game-coloured geode
of a cleaved girl, thrown
to the grass, that blunt mystery.
Look –
the garden is littered.
You can stomach peroxide
if it's ammonia-
free.

## Salome, Herod, Mariamne

*after Mariamne Leaving the Judgement*
*Seat of Herod by J.W.Waterhouse*


Be rock Herod, in your resolve. Hard
as the Masada and the rock beyond
the fortress. Unyielding, postscript of the Dead

Sea as viewed from the tableland:
long marble line which cannot withdraw,
exuding suspension

in sore, corrupted sighs. Three years
in your asylum have left me enlightened.
The stories I could tell! How she was with us –

the duration, of course, but also . . . absent.
Well disposed? Well no, I cannot lie.
And didn't she quake

with silent yearning for the outside,
stirred by the slaves
as they snaked an invisible path

from the gold tread of cisterns,
buckets trembling, more than their lives worth
to spill a drop. If you should waver,

Herod: consider how she disparaged me,
could not see the strategy
in the bloodshed, felt only loss

for her family. Never trust one
who sees detail in the vista,
the fissures and cleft palates of the Desert,

impious colours of the agama
flaring out like lewd tongues from the cracks.
That kind will come undone.

And if you fear me partial in my portrayal,
what of this: the self-portrait
she sent Mark Anthony to pleasure himself to!

Years in your palace of dust
and broken crockery have calloused me.
For this I am grateful. I beg:

heed my counsel. She will poison you
before long. We've come too far
to give up now. Be rock, Herod, be strong.

# The Snow Queen's Factory

Windowless; made Gothic by its blackness.
I wanted to leave but the bus shot off,
truculent against packed snow.
Miles from town,
midwinter.
We had nowhere else to go.

We filed up the path, teeth chattering,
holding onto each other for balance.
Two shovels
crossed in a coat of arms.
Her initials hung on the door:
serpentine, silver-blue.

Our employer was elusive.
It was the glare of two men
that guided our pens on the dotted line,
handed us overalls. We were condomed up,
our hair netted like a heavy haul of fish.

We sealed up slivers of chicken –
the bags decked with smiling roosters.
Under our thin gloves the meat
made a last-ditch squelch toward viscera.
We watched our collective breath
haunt the procession down the belt.

Days went by in an opiate whirr of machinery.
Someone had tightened the vice of the night
so morning and home time

were the same slice of monochrome.
At break we would watch the sundown,
staring mutely at the pink spread like abstract art.
Snow ploughs twinkled like dragons in the distance.

At home, we lay under our husbands,
stiff as Hitchcock blondes,
imagining blink-clear constellations through the ceiling.
If they noticed something wrong they didn't let on:
the money rolled in, the health care.
The grey tide of Mondays.

Our children looked at us, at first in bewilderment,
then indictment. They pulled our sleeves
as if trying to tug us out of ourselves.
We loved our children. They smashed
into our silence like birds.
They stared into our faces like wells.
"We love our children,"
our voices like smothered bells.

One day our toil was interrupted.
A loudspeaker announcement:
She was to come.
We wanted very much to see her.
The place was plastered with posters:
an abstraction of lips and cheekbones,
a workforce observed by her Pop art face:
precise and delicious and vague.

We went outside,
assembled in a neat line:
a long stich of women against the stark white.
The limousine pulled up.
We began chanting the company mantra in a uniform
    refrain:

The cold keeps everything the same
The cold keeps everything the same

# Sister Agnieszka Is Taken with a Dean Martin Impersonator on the Las Vegas Strip

## (PART ONE)

Sister A was rattled. All round the casino –
the stannic clatter of plastic dropping in trays.
She'd observed the routine before each hard waterfall:
one arm jerking repeatedly till the slot's whirling visions
stuck and aligned: three bells or three bullions,
shiny red testicle cherries. Now she bore witness
to an almighty din as the bandits dumped their stash, bang
 on cue.
A man looked up at her, keen as a dog, thinking it divine
 intervention.
If it was, Agnieszka felt short-changed. She'd stopped hoping
for Hail Marys years ago but, come on, where was the joy?
Glum men with shirtfuls of jackpot, waddling like clowns to
 cashiers.
This place was timeless though the roulette wheel wound
like a crazy clock or someone aping the concept of crazy
 with their finger.

Sister rushed past the betters and croupiers,
the tray-bearing waiters, the table laid out
with wound-smelling charcuterie.
She raced down a hallway
revealed in stark phases
by stuttering lamps.
At the end

a red velvet curtain
behind which
the balm
for all of life's wrong:
glorious
subaquatic
snatches of
song

# Notes

The 'Sister Agnieszka' featured throughout this collection is not based on the Agatha Christie character of the same name. I only found out this after writing the poems – just one of those coincidences!

'Interview with The Woman who Trepanned Herself' is inspired by but not directly about Amanda Fielding, an advocate of trepanation who in the seventies drilled a hole into her skull. The narrator of the poem is entirely fictional and is not supposed to be Joseph Cox who interviewed Fielding in 2013 for Vice.

'Notable Globsters' – two of these globsters are "real". One I made up. Or did I?

'The King who Ate Himself to Death' is based on Adolf Frederick, King of Sweden who died in 1771 after consuming a huge feast just before Lent. Among the delicacies he enjoyed were lobster, kippers, caviar and champagne and the meal was topped off by his favourite treat – semla: a sweet roll served in hot milk. He was by all accounts a useless king but a really nice bloke. And what a way to go!

'Kay' is the little boy kidnapped by the Snow Queen in the Hans Christian Andersen fairy tale (sometimes his name is written as Kai).

'Jaws' – The poem is about the henchman in the Bond films (as opposed to the shark!)

'Aviary' – Jean-Eugène Robert-Houdin (1805–1871) was a French magician regarded as the "father of modern conjuring". He initially trained as a watchmaker and was famed in part for his mechanical tricks and automata.

'Jean Harlow, Black Dahlia, Norma Jean' – One of the causes of Jean Harlow's death was said to be uremic poisoning. Elizabeth Short AKA the Black Dahlia was brutally murdered in 1947, her corpse found mutilated and bisected at the waist. Her killer was never found.

# Acknowledgements

Some of these poems have first appeared in the following publications: *Adjacent Pineapple*, *The Dark Horse*, *Glasgow Review of Books*, *Magma*, *New Writing Scotland*, *The North*, *The Ogilvie*, *Shorelines of Infinity*, *One Hand Clapping*, *SOGO*, *Spark: Poems and Artwork inspired by the Novels of Muriel Spark* (Blue Diode Press, 2018), The Vers Prize anthology.

*If Ines* came second in the Singapore Unbound poetry competition 2018.

I am hugely grateful to the Scottish Book Trust for a New Writers Award in poetry 2016 and their invaluable support since then.

Thanks to Chris, Jen and all the team at Salt publishing.

Many thanks to Cheryl Follon, Rob. A Mackenzie, Lindsey Shields Waters for their close reading of this manuscript and for their immense support in everything poetry related and otherwise. Likewise, I am eternally grateful to Nancy Somerville and the Diggers Writers (past and present) for their constructive criticism of the poems, friendship and laughter all the way. A big thank you to the much missed Paul de Havilland and my friend Arthur Allan.

Thanks to John Carson and Jim Aitken for all their encouragement and support when I first started writing and in the years since.

With love and thanks to Mum, Dad, Greg and my family, Rob, my beautiful besties Rach and Babs, the wee wonders Freya and Poppy and all my fantastic friends. You are all stars and I should thank you all much more often. Hope you all know how much I appreciate you.

Thanks to all the tingly literature, music, art and films that helped shiver out these poems from the jar.

This book has been typeset by
SALT PUBLISHING LIMITED
using Sabon, a font designed by Jan Tschichold
for the D. Stempel AG, Linotype and Monotype Foundries.
It is manufactured using Holmen Book Cream 65gsm,
a Forest Stewardship Council™ certified paper from the
Hallsta Paper Mill in Sweden. It was printed and bound
by Clays Limited in Bungay, Suffolk, Great Britain.

CROMER
GREAT BRITAIN
MMXX